ALERTING KIDS TO THE DANGER OF
SEXUAL ABUSE

WRITTEN BY JOY BERRY
Pictures by Bartholomew

Copyright © Joy Berry, 2022
Originally Published, 1984

All rights are reserved.

No part of this book can be duplicated or used without the prior written permission of the copyright owner, except for the use of brief quotations from the book.

For inquiries or permission requests contact the publisher.

Published by Joy Berry Enterprises
www.joyberryenterprises.com

Attention Parents and Teachers

What you don't know CAN hurt you!
People used to believe that children should be kept ignorant for their own sake. In our rapidly changing world, this simply isn't realistic any more. Your children need to know as much as they can about life and its **danger zones**. Since their imaginations can create fantasies worse than any actual situation, they need correct and comprehensible information. The more children know, the better they will be able to protect themselves should they encounter a dangerous situation.

All responsible, caring adults want children to be safe. Unfortunately, our society is becoming increasingly unsafe for children. Young people are being sexually abused in their homes, at day care centers, schools, camps, and other "safe" places. Recent statistics estimate that
- one out of every four girls and one out of every ten boys will be sexually abused before the age of eighteen.
- 75 percent of all crimes against children are sexual in nature.
- 90 percent of sexual abusers are known by their victims.

The problem of sexual abuse has reached epidemic proportions in our country and affects children of all economic classes. Sexual abuse is not something that doesn't happen to "nice" families or in "good" neighborhoods. The statistics quoted above indicate there is a chance that your children could become the victims of sexual abuse or that someone they know will be.

What can you do to help prevent these senseless and abhorrent incidents? Give your children the information they need to avoid being sexually abused. This book provides simple explanations that children can understand. It lists preventive measures along with practical steps to take in a dangerous situation.

Read this book with your children and make sure they understand it. Ask them if they have any questions. Then answer their questions openly and honestly. By doing these things, you are taking an essential step toward ensuring your children's safety. Their awareness of the problem and their knowledge of precautionary techniques can be their best protection.

The back of this book contains important information for parents and teachers. This section includes safety guidelines that you can follow to help protect your children.

This material is not intended to frighten you or your children. The point of this book is to turn fear into healthy caution and to empower young people to remain safe, happy, and free.

Every person's body is special.

There are parts of your body that are your **private parts**. They are called private parts because most people keep them covered most of the time.

A boy's private parts include his
- penis,
- scrotum (testicles), and
- anus.

A girl's private parts include her
- vulva (including the labia and clitoris),
- vagina,
- anus, and
- breasts.

There are some people who might not respect
your right to keep your body safe.
They might make you do something
that involves your private parts.
Or, they might make you do something
that involves their private parts.
If they trick or force you to do this,
it is called **sexual abuse.**

A person who sexually abuses someone is called a **sexual abuser.**

There are several ways people can sexually abuse others.

Some sexual abusers **expose** themselves. They try to show their private parts to other people.

Some sexual abusers **fondle other people.**
They try to touch or stroke
the private parts of others.

Why is he touching me there?

Some sexual abusers try to get other people to **fondle them**. They trick or force people to touch or stroke their private parts.

Some sexual abusers try to trick or force others into having **sexual intercourse.** They try to put their private parts into other people.
Or, they make other people put their private parts into them.

A **sexually abused victim** is a person who is tricked or forced into sexual contact, such as
- exposing,
- fondling, or
- intercourse.

A sexually abused victim can be hurt in many ways.

PHYSICAL HARM
Sometimes sexual abuse can injure a victim's private parts.

EMOTIONAL HARM

Sexual abuse can make victims feel bad.
They might feel <u>helpless</u> because they could not stop the abuse.
They might feel <u>fearful</u> because they are afraid that someone
will find out what happened and will reject or punish them.
They might feel <u>angry</u> that such a thing happened to them.
They might feel <u>guilty</u> if they know that what happened was wrong.

MENTAL HARM

Sexual abuse can confuse victims.
Often they are told by the abuser that sexual contact between them is OK.
Sometimes the victims feel good because the abuser is giving them attention.
At the same time, they might feel bad
if they know that what is happening is wrong.
Feeling good and bad at the same time can be confusing.
Confusion can keep a person from thinking normally.

"I was so confused..."

"Of course you were."

SOCIAL HARM

Sexually abused victims often want to be alone. They might not want to be around other people because they feel embarrassed and ashamed about what happened.

Sexually abused victims might also have a hard time trusting other people. It might become difficult for them to know who to trust and who not to trust.

SEXUAL HARM

Sexual abuse is not normal behavior.
It often gives the victim a bad feeling about sexual experiences.
This feeling might keep the victim from
having a normal sexual relationship.

There are at least eight ways that sexual abusers get their victims to cooperate.

1. FRIENDSHIP
Some sexual abusers act friendly toward their victims. They give their victims attention and affection. In turn, they expect their victims to trust them and to do what they say.

"We're best friends. I want us to do this because we love each other."

2. WITHHOLDING

Some sexual abusers are responsible for the care of others. The people that they take care of can become their victims. If their victims do not cooperate, the abusers can easily withhold important things that the victims want or need.

3. BRIBES
Some sexual abusers bribe their victims.
They give their victims gifts or they promise to do favors so that their victims will cooperate.

5. TRICKS

Some sexual abusers trick their victims. They deceive them into going away with them. Or, the abusers trick their victims into believing it is OK to be with them and to do what they say.

The other kids I invited couldn't come. So we're going to be alone together.

6. INTIMIDATION

Some sexual abusers intimidate their victims. The victims are made to believe that they're
- helpless,
- weak, or
- inferior.

This makes the victims feel that they must cooperate with the abusers.

He's an adult. I'm supposed to obey adults. If I don't do what he says, he could hurt me.

8. FORCE
Some sexual abusers use physical strength to overpower their victims. They force their victims to cooperate.

Remember that there are at least eight ways that sexual abusers get their victims to cooperate. They use
- friendship,
- withholding,
- bribes,
- games,
- tricks,
- intimidation,
- threats, and
- force.

No matter how sexual abusers get their victims to cooperate, they tell their victims to keep it a secret. The abusers do not want others to know about it because they know that sexual abuse is wrong. They do not want to get into trouble for what they have done.

Sometimes the relationship between sexual abusers
and their victims takes a long time to develop.
At first the abusers do not do
very much to their victims,
but as time passes they do more and more.

"At first, he just wanted me to hug him, but later he wanted to touch my private parts."

Sometimes abusers sexually abuse their victims the first time they are together.

Some victims are abused only once.
Some may be abused several times.
Others may be abused many times.

There are several reasons why people sexually abuse others.

Some abusers have mental problems.
They have minds that do not function normally.
These people are not able to think and act like most people their age.

Some sexual abusers were abused when they were younger.
They are still angry about being abused.
They express their anger by abusing others.

Some abusers feel inferior. They want to dominate others. They sexually abuse smaller or weaker people so that they can feel more important.

"I'm tired of people thinking they're better than I am."

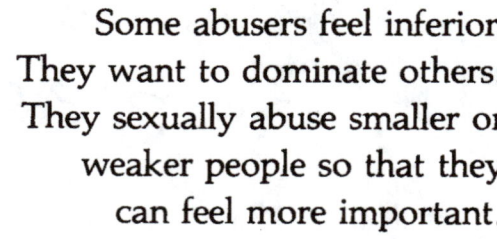

Some sexual abusers have emotional problems.
They are not able to handle the stress in their lives.
They express their frustration by sexually abusing other people.

No matter what the reason, sexual abuse is against the law.
This law applies to everyone.

There are many ways you can keep yourself safe from sexual abuse.

AVOID STRANGERS
Do not talk to them.
Do not go anywhere with them.
Do not take things from them.
Do not play with them.
Do not be alone with them.

I don't know this guy! I'm getting out of here!

AVOID PEOPLE WHO YOU SUSPECT WANT TO HAVE SEXUAL CONTACT WITH YOU

Do not talk to them.
Do not go anywhere with them.
Do not take things from them.
Do not play with them.
Do not be alone with them.

SAY "NO!"
If other people want to show you their private parts, say "NO!"
If other people want to touch your private parts, say "NO!"
If other people want you to touch their private parts, say "NO!"
If other people want to put their private parts inside you, say "NO!"

There are many ways to say "NO!"
You can say "NO!" with words such as
- "Don't do that."
- "I don't want to."
- "I'm not supposed to do this."
- "I'm going to tell on you if you don't stop."

You can also say "NO!" with actions such as **screaming, yelling,** or **running away.**

TALK TO SOMEONE

If a person has sexually abused you or tried to abuse you, tell someone about it immediately.
Choose a person you trust.
Choose someone who cares about you.
Make sure it is someone who is old enough and wise enough to help you.

Tell the person everything that happened. It is important for the person who helps you to have complete information.

Dad, I need to talk to you.

Some people may not believe you.
If the person you tell doesn't help you,
talk to another person.
<u>Keep talking to people</u>
<u>until you find someone to help you.</u>

Being sexually abused can make you feel bad for a long time, but it does not have to make you feel bad forever.
Here are some things you can do to help yourself if you have been sexually abused.

DON'T BLAME YOURSELF
Remember that it is not your fault
that you were sexually abused.
The person who abused you is to blame.
The abuser broke the law.
You are not to blame.

It's not my fault.
I'm not to blame
for what happened.

Now you're
on the right track.

ACCEPT YOUR FEELINGS

If you have been sexually abused, you will probably feel
- helpless,
- angry,
- fearful, and
- guilty.

These are normal reactions. Try not to think there is something wrong with you for feeling the way you feel.
It is important for you
to talk about your feelings.
Talking to someone who cares about you
will make you feel better.

It's normal for you to feel the way you are feeling...

GET HELP FROM PROFESSIONALS

There are many professional people who can help you. A caring adult can get you to a doctor if you have been physically harmed. This person can also notify special people in your community, such as a police officer or a child protection worker. These people will make sure that the abuser does not continue to abuse you. A caring adult can also get a counselor or therapist to help you understand and get over what has happened. With the help of these people, you can feel good about yourself again.

. . . and I'm glad you talked to me. Let's go see some people who can help you.

Now that you know about sexual abuse,
you and your friends can help prevent it.

Remember...

WE HAVE THE RIGHT TO KEEP OUR BODIES SAFE!

Important Information for Parents and Teachers

Myths About Sexual Abuse

Myth: Sexual abusers are usually strangers to their victims.

In nine out of ten cases, assailants are known by their victims. Sexual abusers can be primary caretakers, other relatives, neighbors, teachers, and professionals who work with children.

Myth: Incidents of child sexual abuse are always reported to the police.

Few incidents are reported. Actual figures are difficult to obtain. However, in cases of adult rape, conservative FBI estimates indicate that one out of three rapes is reported. If the abuser is a relative of a child victim, it is even less likely that the incident will be reported.

Myth: Sexual abuse of children is usually violent, and physical trauma is the greatest harm resulting from this kind of abuse.

Violent attacks and forced penetration of the victim occur in only 5 percent of reported cases. The abuser often finds it easy to trick a child into sexual contact. Bribes and affection are the most effective tools of the sexual abuser. Psychological and emotional harm is the most devastating effect of sexual abuse of children.

Myth: Children make up stories about being sexually abused.

It is very rare that a child lies about sexual abuse. Often children have been told by their abusers that no one will believe their story. Therefore, children need support and comfort when they disclose what has happened to them. They need to be reassured that they are believed and that someone will help them.

Myth: Some children act seductively and want to have sexual relations with adults.

Children never ask to be sexually abused. While some children may be looking for affection or responding to it, the responsibility rests with the offender, not the victim. This also applies to cases where the abuser is someone the child knows or even loves.

Myth: Children never get over the harm of sexual abuse.

In cases where violent physical harm did not occur and where the assailant does not have a close relationship with the victim, children recover faster than adult victims. The most important factor in children's recovery is how appropriately the incident is handled by the adults who surround them.

To Fight or Not to Fight

A decision all parents must make is whether to teach their children to aggressively defend themselves against attackers. There are two schools of thought on this.

1. By kicking, hitting, and biting, kids can startle their attacker and get away.
2. Such actions only anger the attacker and could cause children to be hurt.

This book does not advocate aggressive self-defense for the following reasons:

- Keeping the assault as nonviolent as possible reduces the chance of the child getting hurt or even killed.
- Since the majority of assaults on children are nonviolent, assertive behavior such as saying "no" and running away is more appropriate than fighting.
- There is no way of knowing whether or not an attacker has a weapon. Fighting back could cause the attacker to react by using a weapon that is concealed.
- Self-defense training can give children a false sense of security. Instead of being cautious, they might